MY CRYSTAL ROMANCE

Brandon Chatagnier

May 2018

Copyright © 2019 by Brandon Chatagnier.

ISBN: 978-1-7338565-0-8

All rights reserved. No part of this book may be reproduced or transmitted in any form or by any means, electronic or mechanical, including photocopying, recording, or by any information storage and retrieval system, without permission in writing from the copyright owner. This is a work of fiction. Names, characters, places and incidents either are the product of the author's imagination or are used fictitiously, and any resemblance to any actual persons, living or dead, events, or locales is entirely coincidental. This book was printed in the United States of America.

To order additional copies of this book, contact:
Brandon Chatagnier
P.O. Box 967
Tioga La. 71477
E-Mail: bredeemed75@gmail.com

Foreword

Years of rebellion, pain and heartache followed Brandon as he fought against God's perfect will for his life. He fell into a world of addiction and hit rock bottom. Then he finally looked up and heard the call from the Lord as his family and friends steadily prayed for his recovery.

His renewed spiritual walk reflects a more positive, encouraging, and strong man of God; one who desires to help others struggling in the same areas of addiction. Blessed with five beautiful daughters and his loving new wife, they all continue to pray and work with him as he follows this new path God has for him.

Words can't express how proud we are of Brandon Chatagnier's walk with the Lord. We are excited to see what God has in store for him in this new era of his life while he displays his determination to follow God's perfect will.

God bless you, Brandon Chatagnier, in all you do.

Tommy and Marilyn Blalock

"MEETING CRYSTAL"

CHAPTER 1

We were both young then. She was an amazing girl, but I brought to the table a pretty high level of immaturity. As with most young people in their late teens and early twenties, we thought we were the only ones in the world who had ever been in love. The experience would teach us that we had a lot to learn about love and life.

Throughout seven years, our love and marriage gifted us with three astonishing and amazing daughters: Magan, Haley, and Alyssa. During most of that time, she was both an amazing mother and wife. I was not a good father, and certainly not a good husband. From day one, I knew I had married up; and that I never deserved her. While I claimed to love her more than life itself, I didn't do much to keep her love for me alive. I was inattentive to her and the girls, and selfish and self-centered in most of what I said and did.

Eventually, she'd had enough. She said the words no man ever wants to hear: "I don't love you anymore." And with that, she was gone. My world began to crumble.

At this juncture, it would be easy to blame what happened next on her. After all, she left me. I was devastated. However, I am smarter than that, and hopefully wiser than that. What happened next was no one's fault but my own.

My Crystal Romance

Depression set in. I had lost everything that truly mattered to me. Against everything I knew and had ever been taught, I turned to alcohol. It became my gateway to decades of dabbling in alcohol and a variety of drugs.

Let me interrupt here with just a little background information on the earlier years of my life. I was adopted days after I was born by a dedicated Christian couple. From day one, they provided for me everything I could need or want. Not only did they provide for my physical needs, but they also made sure that I was taken to church and taught the Bible and the things of the Kingdom of God. I attended church camps during the summer. I rarely, if ever, missed Sunday school – or

My Crystal Romance

Sunday-night service – or Wednesday-night Bible Study. If there was a revival, we were there. I had felt the power of God and known the power of prayer. When faced with the devastation of my life, something in me turned away from all of that and chose a different path.

I knew there would be way too many restrictions should I try to move in with my parents. Consequently, I moved in with my best friend and his wife. There were no guidelines at their house. They accepted my broken heart and broken life, and understood that clubbing – the cycle of nightly drinking and the addition of one medication or another – was helping me numb my pain. Clubbing was also a part of my search for another girl to fill the void left by losing my wife and my family. Little did I know where my search would lead me.

One night, at a party, I met the perfect girl. She filled the void, at least temporarily. I was drunk and high from the pills I had taken. The combination of alcohol and pills had left me agitated and unruly.

A friend of mine said, "Here, Brandon… this will help you out." He laid out a line of something on the counter. "Snort this line, and it will sober you up."

I remember asking if it was cocaine.

"No, it's meth."

My Crystal Romance

My romance with a girl named Crystal began. I had never heard of her before that night. I had no idea what devastation and destruction she would leave in my life.

I picked up the straw, put it to my nose, and snorted the line. It was the worst decision of my life. Crystal, my new girlfriend, has been labeled by some as the most powerful drug on Earth. There was a burning pain that seemed to shoot through my nose all the way to the back of my brain. I watched in the mirror as my pupils dilated instantly. Then I felt it start to "drip" into my system.

Not only did I become sober almost instantly, it was as if no alcohol had been consumed. I was euphorically high and focused. In six steps between the bathroom counter and the door, I became the man every little boy imagines himself to be when he's wearing a towel around his shoulders and playing Superman in the backyard. Nothing was impossible for me. No one could even come close to being the person I had just become.

As I looked around the house, I seemed to have developed some keen insight into furniture placement and décor. I suddenly saw the beauty in everything, from the placement of a chair to a wall hanging. Colors were more vibrant than I had ever seen. Suddenly, I was smarter than anyone else in the room.

I wanted to go back to school and become a doctor – a brain surgeon or a cardiologist – or maybe both! I wanted to go back to every failed job on my resume, and become the CEO of the company in a month. There was also a sense of physical empowerment. I had never before felt as amazing as I did at that moment. I could do anything! The physical feeling was so awesome. These are all just the drug's effects on the human mind and body. It was so powerful and so incredibly amazing that when it wore off the next day, I didn't want to live any more of my life without it. The reality was so drastically different. I seemed to feel every failure, disappointment, and pain I had ever felt in my life all coming back at once. Despair could take my breath away.

So I found myself doing all I could to never come down while trying to maintain my job in my parents' business, a local restaurant. I remember one particular night. We were swamped. I rang the bell to send out an order while simultaneously dropping another basket of fish into the fryer, putting plenty of fries and hush puppies on deck, and setting the plates up for my next five orders. I swung out to the crawfish porch to check on the orders there. In what seemed like two minutes, I had done all of that – and checked on the customers in the dining room as well. I checked with the wait staff, and was back in the kitchen just in time to pull the basket of fish before they overcooked. Now, all of that may seem somewhat routine and normal for a capable and efficient worker. However, for a young man like me, who was diagnosed with "the worst case of ADHD ever seen" by my doctor, it was a feat that would have been impossible without my friend, Crystal.

CHAPTER 2

I did well in hiding my "relationship" with Crystal... or so I thought.

At first, the only people who knew about my budding addiction were my dealer, my best friend, and me. I had a pretty set routine that allowed me to fool most of the people who might be observing me into believing I had just turned over a new leaf, like what everyone talks about. I would work a few hours, slip into the restroom and do a line of meth, work a few more hours, then throw a piece on some foil to smoke. The one thing I didn't do was allow my supply to run out; I could not and would not stop using.

The reality was that life – with all its responsibilities, emotions, fears, faults, and failures – was my enemy. I feared facing reality more than anything else I could imagine in life. I would get off work and go to my house behind the restaurant, take a shower, and then rush to get to my dealer's house (which was about 25 miles away) to buy what I needed to get me through the next few days. On most days, I paid for the drugs with money I had pocketed from the restaurant's register. I would then hurry back home alone, lock all the doors, and sit down and smoke meth all night long. I never realized I had become a virtual recluse. I could go a full week – and sometimes,

My Crystal Romance

even longer – without eating or sleeping much at all.

I still don't know just when my family began to suspect that something was wrong. I tried continuing to do everything I used to. I attended family gatherings. I was able to keep my job, though probably because my mother was my boss. I was functioning well; I was also functioning high, and believing no one could tell. I justified every single shard of crystal I used by telling myself I wasn't hurting anyone. It just made me a much better version of myself.

Slowly but surely, I started meeting other people who did meth (tweakers) and began to spend more time with them. It wasn't long until I was getting meth for all of them. Then one night, while at my plug (my dealer)'s house, getting a gram for whatever price they were going for at that time, I overheard a transaction between him and another customer. He was selling him a much more significant amount, but the numbers didn't add up.

I went home and looked for a calculator. I quickly punched in the numbers, and discovered something that rapidly led to the second worst decision I ever made in my life: becoming the seller and buyer. I called my plug and asked why there was a price difference. He explained, "'Cuz he sells it. He buys a lot more than you do." I wished he'd just said, "'Cuz I like him more" and hung up on me.

I wasted no time calling a new yet close friend of mine whom I knew was friends with the biggest dealer around at that time. Within 24 hours, I found myself sitting in a shop with her at a desk, waiting for him to meet me. It was one of those moments I would never forget. He came in with a five-gallon bucket in one hand and a MAK II UZI submachine gun in the other. He sat the bucket on the floor and the UZI on the desk. Before sitting down, he leaned across the desk toward me and said, "If you ever talk about me or screw me over, I'll kill you!" Naturally, I immediately agreed not to.

He sat down, popped the lid off the bucket, and said: "She tells me you can move a lot of meth." My jaw must have dropped when I saw that the bucket was filled to the brim with meth. At that time, the street value was probably somewhere around $250,000.

The rest of that discussion and transaction is just details. However, I can tell you that on that night, I became one of only five guys who were dealers for our community's biggest supplier at that time. You have to understand that in this small, rural Louisiana town, that gives a person "rock star" status among the known population of meth users in that area. When you combine that with the effects that your personal drug use has on you,

My Crystal Romance

you feel like a superstar. Your mind is warped. Logical thinking is absent from any equation. It's easy to believe that everyone loves you rather than the meth you bring. When every girl wants you and every guy wants to be you, the lifestyle becomes equally or even more addictive than the drug.

In six months, I went from being a lonely, heartbroken, divorced nobody to what seemed to be the most desired, popular and influential guy among everyone I knew. In no way, form or fashion was that a good thing. I was now deeply in love with this new demon in my life, and there would be no turning back.

It wasn't long until ecstasy and cocaine came along and became a part of my life as well. Although my soapbox is meth, I have to put a strong warning out against ecstasy. I've always said that "They don't call it ecstasy for no reason." It's probably the most physically, emotionally and euphorically amazing drug out there. I always swore to myself that I wouldn't sugarcoat or hide that fact – not to encourage its use, but to let people know how easy it is to fall in love with and further destroy yourself. Night after night of using ecstasy and meth turned into week after week and caused me to have to push so much more meth that eventually, the lifestyle overtook and consumed me.

My Crystal Romance

There were times when I would drive up to 900 miles in a day, trying to get to all the people who wanted what I had. It became so crazy. A 24-hour period of my life consisted of getting extremely high on meth, picking up my phone, going through sometimes 600 calls and texts from a hundred different people, seeing how much meth I needed to take care of all of them, and then heading out to "re-up" (the term used for restocking one's supply). This consisted of going to a very private place, home, shop, or other location; and spending an hour visiting and getting higher with my supplier. Then it was back into the car and going nonstop for literally 20 hours, hitting every spot unnecessarily.

My Crystal Romance

I always timed it so I would be finished in time to re-up again and be home at 3:00-4:00 in the morning, hopefully with a girl. But more often than not, I was alone or with a few friends. I'd shower, dress and try to relax for an hour or so while getting high again, only to pick up my phone at daylight and start the process all over again. This would usually go on for 7-10 days before I would shut down for 12 hours and sleep.

That in itself was a major ordeal. When I'd go that long and hard without stopping things and taking a break, people would pile up on me. I'd have accumulated six or eight people in my house, each one getting high on my stuff for free, simply

My Crystal Romance

because they were each connected to a different group of people to whom I sold meth.

It is a world unto itself. Everyone keeps secrets, and are private about what they are doing and with whom they are doing it. I would not sell meth to anyone new unless they were referred to me by someone I trusted. A "new" client had to make their purchases through someone I trusted several times before I would consider selling to them directly. That seems to have changed now. The end user is so afraid of being known that they won't buy from someone they don't know unless it's done through someone they trust. No one trusts anyone in the meth game.

CHAPTER 3

At any rate, I had a very life- and time-consuming addiction to the drug. At this point in my life, I think my addiction became more toward the lifestyle of dealing than with the actual using.

In the beginning, I was addicted to the drug for the feeling of being high, and the enjoyment of what it did for me. After I started dealing meth, the reason for my addiction changed. I can only recall there ever being about six or eight hours every two weeks that I used meth for personal enjoyment. The rest of the time, I stayed high only to stay awake and keep going for as long as necessary to keep up with all the business.

Looking back, I can't remember at what point it stopped being fun. I remember it being very stressful. You cannot believe how addictive it can be to be that in demand, and feel that wanted and needed. People have "sold their soul to the devil" to live how I was living. I never sold my soul for it. I believe this is where the grace of God in my life came into play. I had given my life to Christ at age 12. I had certainly done a lot of things that would make you think that negotiation was null and void. The God I serve is relentless in His love for His children. He came to seek and save the lost . . . And as long as I was lost, He was seeking me.

My Crystal Romance

There is an elder minister whom I have been privileged to know for most of my life. He has a saying: "Sin will take you further than you want to go, keep you longer than you want to stay, and cost you more than you ever intended to pay." My life became so much darker and more profound than I ever imagined it could be. I went to places where the feeling of spiritual wickedness and evil was so strong, it sent chills down my spine. It is only now I realize that even though I was walking in such an evil world, it was the power of the prayers prayed for me by my parents and other friends – and the grace of God – that protected me. As ironic as it sounds, there were times when

My Crystal Romance

I believe God alerted me to those dangerous circumstances and evil spirits.

In one incident, I walked into a place and felt an evil and demonic presence around me. It was a month later when I discovered that the girl I had met there had been involved in killing her husband in that very place. The spirits of evil and death remained.

Later, I would hear a story going around that the guy I had become friends with was allegedly involved in dismembering her husband's body and helping dispose of it. I still get chills while writing about it.

I had similar experiences twice in 15 years with two different girls I dated. It was during the times

I was with them when I remembered feeling demonic spirits and presences around me. I didn't immediately connect that with the girls, but rather with the circumstances of my life at the time. Then, long after I dated them, I learned they had both been somehow involved in the deaths of their respective husbands.

The rush and curiosity that comes with being in places filled with such an evil and dark presence were impossible to walk away from. It was like watching a horror movie or documentary on possessed places. The incredible desire to know what was behind that feeling of such spiritual darkness was so strong, I couldn't walk out. It drew me in.

As days, weeks, and months went by, I felt further and further from God; and those demonic feelings became so predominant in my life that I was very close to being numb to them. Satan was in complete control at this point. I hated going to church because I felt so wrong for it. I was drawn to that holy place, if for no other reason to make sure I could still feel God. I desperately wanted to leave because I felt the Spirit of God drawing me in once I got there. The enemy had so much control over me during that time that I would fight desperately to hold back tears of surrender. I just couldn't let go of the life that was waiting for me outside the church doors. Eventually, it had gone on for so long and it had such control over me that

My Crystal Romance

I couldn't remember how to live the way I used to before meth. Now, this was the only way of life I seemed to know. I couldn't remember being clean.

I cannot put into words how terrible it feels to miss five amazing daughters, yet hate going around them because of the pain I would feel whenever I had to leave them again to go back into the world that now owned me. I knew for sure that I never wanted them to see that world or be a part of it, nor see me in it.

The most powerful gods of this world – meth, sex, and popularity – always seemed to win, at least in my world. They may have different names for someone else, but these were mine. Still, to this

My Crystal Romance

day, I shudder when I remember the things I missed with my girls. There are hours of homework help, after-school stories, bedtime prayers, and breakfast dreams that I missed and will never regain. There are thousands of "butterfly kisses" I missed. I may be their father; but for all practical purposes, all we shared was the biology. For 14 years, this was my struggle – and drugs and dealing won over fathering and family every time.

Somewhere in there, I met a girl. She will remain nameless. However, for the next few years, she became everything to me. We were inseparable. We were Bonnie and Clyde #1 for me (because there would be a #2). She had a family history of crime and involvement in the underworld. We were so in sync; she knew exactly what to say and what to do, and when to be more and more a part of my life. We quickly got to that couple stage of being able to finish each other's sentences. She was ride-or-die since day one. I finally thought I was in love again; in fact, all I was doing was reverting to enjoying the meth, ecstasy, and sex. I had someone to share in the burden and responsibilities of the dealing aspect of my life.

During this time frame, ecstasy became the everyday drug of choice; and my use of meth tripled. I lost a lot during those few years because all I was willing to deal meth for was to come up with just enough to stay high on ecstasy and meth

My Crystal Romance

with her at home for days on end. The meth was so strong, the ecstasy was so engulfed with passion, and she became one more addiction for me. I used to say that she infected me. She was the lifeblood that ran through my veins. I soon found out how strong lust could be. Now Satan had one more string with which to control me as my puppeteer.

Within this period, I think I put my life on the line more times than ever. I was playing with death daily. I was pushing the envelope daily with how much meth and "X" I used. The amounts I used were lethal, but they were the only way I could get the rush I needed. Then I started combining them with violent physical actions to push my adrenaline to the point that (along with the drugs in my system) it should have killed me on many occasions.

There is a thing people do on ecstasy called "passing out" that is dangerous in itself. It's a form of strangulation, done by taking a series of fast, deep breaths; then taking a deep breath and squeezing your neck tight enough to stop the blood flow to the brain just long enough until you pass out. In doing so, you release the pressure to your neck; and the blood rushes back to the brain, bringing you "back to". You are usually out for only ten seconds or so, but coming "back to" while being very high on ecstasy ("rolling") and having your blood flooding back to your brain is a mighty rush. When done in the dark with some form of colorful flashing lights and loud techno music, it is a rush so powerful that you feel as though you are coming out of a journey that lasted hours.

Because this technique is so strong, it has caused people's hearts to stop. I used to do it so many times while I was rolling that others who rolled with me stayed worried that I would kill myself. I would sneak off and climb onto the roof of my apartment with headphones on and lie down on the roof, looking up at the stars. And I would do it alone, which is very dangerous. However, it seemed to be the only way I could feel that rush of euphoria and emotion I needed.

My Crystal Romance

I remember a time when a friend and I drove down the expressway, with him in the passenger seat, and both of us were rolling on ecstasy very hard. I lied and told him to take the wheel so I could get a CD. Then I threw my head back, grabbed my neck, and passed myself out at 70 mph. I came to a mile and a half later, at a major curve. That's how much I played with death. My survival is just another sign of the power of the grace of God, and the prayers of a godly mother and friends.

The breakup came utterly unexpectedly. It caused me to literally lose all control. I walked in one day and found my girlfriend of two years in bed with a man whom I thought was my friend. I thank God every time I think about it. It was again His grace that kept me from killing one of them. I grabbed him and threw him out of my house. I took her clothes and threw them out as well, leaving her naked and scared, wrapped in a sheet in the bedroom. In a rage, I tore up almost everything in my house that was ours, never letting her out of the room.

Somewhere around 2:00 am, I made her get in the backseat of the car, still naked; and I started driving. I still can't remember if anything was going on in my mind. I don't even remember where I drove to; I remember it was way out in the woods.

I found a clearing that was away from any significant roads. It sickens me every time I think of how scared that girl must have been when I stopped the car, got out, walked to my trunk, and opened it. I'm not sure what I thought was going to be there – or what I thought I was going to do. I stared into a trunk that was empty except for a wadded-up pillowcase in the corner. At that point, I pulled her out of the car and threw the pillowcase at her. I looked at her for a long moment and said, "You don't know how much I loved you." Then, without saying another word, I got in my car and drove off. I didn't go back to check on her.

I have no idea how she got out of those woods, or what happened to her for the rest of that night.

My Crystal Romance

After a few years, we eventually spoke again, but just casually. But there was another time years later when she came to me to apologize for how badly I was hurt in our relationship. I had to admit that I was the one who owed her an apology.

Something was different about the way I handled that situation compared to all the other times I dealt with something while on meth. The difference was the needle. If we rewind about 3-4 months before the breakup, you'll see where I made another very, very bad decision. It had been a long night of partying and getting high; and everyone was gone except me, my girlfriend, and a friend of hers. I walked into the living room and kind of collapsed back into the couch next to them with a sigh of relief. I immediately noticed that the two of them were fooling around with a needle and a spoon, trying to figure out how to shoot up for the first time.

As usual, I just had to be the know-it-all and show them how it was done. I had never done it before either, but they weren't going to know that. I was too cool for that. At one point in my drug life, I had watched a roommate do it so many times, I was pretty sure I knew what to do.

I proceeded to demonstrate. I put a few pieces of what we referred to at the time as "blue ice" into the spoon, along with a couple of drops of water; and mixed it up. I could not have possibly understood the enormity of the change that was about to take place, sitting there in a quiet living room in the wee hours of the morning.

CHAPTER 4

Up to this point, I had only smoked or snorted meth, or taken it by mouth in capsule form. This couldn't be all that different. After all, I seemed to have a higher tolerance at this point than anyone else I knew.

Anyway, I placed the needle in the spoon and drew up this liquid demon. I broke the skin, entered the vein, and pushed the plunger. In less than one second, the drug traveled through my heart, up my neck, and into my brain, choking me with the taste of its chemical fumes.

That was it. I would never be able to get high any other way again. I had just entered the code that

My Crystal Romance

put me in god mode in the dope game. For those of you who don't know what "god mode" is in a video game, it is a cheat mode that gives the player unlimited power, lives, ammo, weapons and, in some games, the ability to walk through the wall to other levels. I don't think I ever walked through any walls, but the meth-induced psychosis sure made me feel like I did at times.

I'll explain it like this: without any drugs, sleep deprivation of only three days can cause a person to hallucinate naturally. The brain becomes so tired that it starts to slip, and reality becomes blurry. Stationary objects seem to start to move or drift. Changing focal points too quickly can cause what you were first looking at to blend in with what you looked at next. This is referred to as seeing shadow figures or shadow monkeys; all shadows seem to come alive. I think every meth user has experienced them at some point. Now, this all starts naturally after about three days without sleep. Add the most powerful speed in the world, and about 10 or 15 days to that, and you have meth-induced psychosis.

Those shadows become the Drug Enforcement Agency (DEA) or a Special Weapons and Tactics (SWAT) team. Before you know it, you have been in the woods for two days, on top of an old and abandoned barn, looking through binoculars made of two Mountain Dew bottles you've taped together because they make everything look

My Crystal Romance

green and you think it's night vision. The shadow-monkey DEA has you surrounded, and you know they are about to take you down at any minute. So what do you do? Take another shot. There's no sense in not getting high before they catch you. The cycle starts all over again, becoming a little more and more retarded each time. It's not all fun. It can scare the hell out of many people who experience it. The power of meth addiction is too strong to break.

I had been using and selling meth, ecstasy, and cocaine for about four years when I shot up for the first time. At that point, I was doing as well as I thought a drug dealer could do. I had two apartments I was paying the rent on. I even had

My Crystal Romance

two cars, and two girlfriends. Even though my money usually went toward the re-up, I never had less than $4,000 in my pocket. I thought I was doing it right.

But putting a needle in my arm was the beginning of a very rapid end. Over the next eight months, I lost everything I had spent four years working for in the dope game. First went my apartments, then one of my cars, then the other. Eventually, my money was gone; my friends disappeared; and finally, even my girlfriend. I think the other losses contributed to my major freak-out when my girlfriend cheated on me, and I realized my last relationship was no more.

For some reason, I thought we would always be together. But God had a different plan. Don't get me wrong; I don't think my drug lifestyle was God's will or plan. However, I do believe He allowed me to experience everything I did for a reason. My mother once said, "Everything happens for a reason and a season." It's true, and that's why wisdom is so important. Knowledge is an accumulation of facts, such as everything I experienced and went through or learned in those four-and-a-half years. Wisdom means knowing what to do with those facts or knowledge. I didn't have much wisdom at that point, obviously; or this book would be a lot shorter than it is because I

My Crystal Romance

would have run as fast as I could away from that life.

Here's how my first battle with meth came to an end. Eight months had gone by since I first shot up meth. I had lost everything. I stopped in at a friend's house, hoping to steal a shower; and was turned down. So I found myself walking down the street with everything I owned in a backpack. It hadn't even occurred to me that this was going to be a game-changing day in my life's story.

I dropped my backpack and sat down on the ground behind the Rapides Parish Coliseum. It was a beautiful sunny day. With tears in my eyes, I dialed the only number that I knew would be answered by a prayer warrior: my mom.

My Crystal Romance

I'll never forget that brief conversation. I said, "Mom, it's over. I need help. I got to get out of this life before it kills me."

She replied, "Where are you? I'm sending someone to get you right now."

I remember how just hearing those words was such a huge relief. The best way I can explain it is like this: You are swimming, and you hold your breath and then swim down as deep as you can. You turn and start swimming back up, only to realize you swam down too far. Panic sets in. You find yourself frantically trying to get back to the surface. You cannot hold your breath a second longer. Finally, you break the surface and take that first, massive gasp of air; and realize that you made it. Gradually, your racing heart rate slows back to normal, and you know you are safe. That's what hearing my mother's words felt like that day: breaking the surface, and beginning to breathe again.

At this point in my life, I have still never thanked my mom – or the next three people I will mention for the love and kindness I received over the next hour and the next month. They were there for me at my lowest, unlike anyone in my life has ever been. I was picked up by Todd Hudspeth, a childhood friend who dropped everything and came. His kindness, prayers, and words of advice were so instrumental; and made an excellent start to my recovery. (Thank you so much, Todd, for

My Crystal Romance

being there for the lowest piece of trash, drug dealer, and addict in town.) He drove me home. My mom and dad were waiting with open arms. My mom had already found help for my next step in recovery.

That's where the second person comes in. For the first month or so of my recovery, he was the one who dealt with the worst-case scenarios of someone getting off drugs. Marvin Poole, another lifelong friend and an awesome pastor, was my rescuer. He pastors a church in Hammond, Louisiana that couldn't be more appropriately named: Soul's Harbor. He took me in without hesitation.

Not only did he take my needs on, but he took me into his home with his wife and beautiful daughters. He let me live with them. From the first day, he never treated me as less than equal. He fed me, gave me my room, and allowed me to roam freely in his home. He stood next to me and prayed me through some very rough detox. He let me work in his house, yard, and church. It wasn't a barter system for him; my work wasn't to cover the expenses for my care. He paid me for my work. He showed me the love and compassion of a true Christian.

Marvin, I love you and Angela, and your houseful of girls. I thank you for showing me Jesus Christ in you during that period in my life. Your true

My Crystal Romance

Christianity is made evident by the way you live the love of Christ to people who don't deserve it. The power of God at work in your life is made evident when you allow Him to work through you in the lives of others. Oh, and don't get too mad, but I have to come clean with you about something that happened while I was there. It was just a little thing. I took your beautiful motorcycle around the block one day while you weren't home.

The last of the three people who helped me was my cousin, Renee Pedigo. She took me in when I left Marvin's and put me to work. She spent countless hours just talking to me and not judging me. Thank you, Renee.

After I had spent a few months with Renee and went back home, I moved in with my parents and started looking for work. During this period, I met the lady who would become my second wife. From our first encounter, I thought she was "the one". I asked her out the first night I met her, and refused to take no for an answer. We went out that night to a club and clicked.

I was not ready for any level of commitment besides where we were in this growing relationship. However, it got fast-tracked fast when she told me, a month into our relationship, that she was pregnant. I knew I wasn't ready for that yet, but I wanted to make the best of the situation.

My Crystal Romance

She and I got married. My fourth child, and her first, was a beautiful baby girl named Patience. I went to work offshore in the oilfield, and things went great from there. I found myself drug-free, married, with a home, two cars, a camper, a swimming pool, and steaks on the grill every weekend. My family was together; I thought I was happy. We all did.

Then my last little girl, Ady, came along. She's been an exceptional and strong little girl. She has a story to tell that we will share later.

Everything seemed to be going smoothly until December 19, 2013. I got laid off at work, and I wasn't the only one. The oilfield took a big hit. I couldn't find work anywhere. We started losing things because the money wasn't coming in. Then, under a lot of stress and depression, she and I decided to get high one night.

I would give anything to go back to that night and not make that decision. Within a few weeks, I was back selling meth in full swing. My second wife became my second ride-or-die girl: Bonnie & Clyde #2. We were so well put together, even the narcotics agents we eventually started having run-ins with tried to trip us up with every sale and couldn't. We went wide open in the dope game. But somehow, I was blind to the fact that my home was no longer a happy one. My marriage was crumbling.

My Crystal Romance

I just couldn't quit selling and using meth, even though she begged me to stop. With the volume of drugs we were personally using, dealing was the only option to cover the expense of it.

It was during this time when I started sneaking off and manufacturing meth. My wife thought I was cheating on her when I would disappear for hours and hours. Even if I knew that lie hurt her, I found myself unable to tell her the truth: that selling had turned to manufacturing.

We ended up getting busted at our home one day. We both went to jail. Our parents took our children to keep them from going into the child-services system. I was convinced that her parents had alerted the law to our activities. I refused to ever live in that home again due to its proximity to their home.

CHAPTER 5

My life was a bigger mess than ever. All my time was going into the dope game – dealing, manufacturing, and using. Meanwhile, she was home alone with two baby girls most of the time. She was constantly accusing me of cheating on her, which I never did. She felt most of the responsibility for the care of our two young daughters. We had no home. I dragged them from one hotel to another, one rented room in a friend's house to another. It was not a life for babies or grownups. It was our life, though; and my addiction blinded me again.

My Crystal Romance

I accumulated 32 bookings into the parish jail with one drug arrest after another. There was always one contempt-of-court charge after another. She and I were constantly fighting. I became a monster – a man I did not recognize.

One night, I got up with her to bring someone some meth; and realized my dope was missing. It was the dope I was planning to sell to get us away from that life.

I completely lost it. I was in a house full of people who were all asleep except for me, my wife, and some girl I didn't know. Missing dope was a big deal. I dragged that girl by her hair outside the house, threatening to kill her if she didn't give me back the dope she had stolen. It created such a ruckus that the whole house was awake before long. I gave up on her and came back into the house. I cut the phone lines to the house and collected cell phones. My next step was going to be a strip search. I desperately wanted my drugs back.

One girl was able to keep her cell phone without me realizing I had missed her. She messaged her mom and told her I was holding the entire house hostage, and that they were afraid for their lives. That mother called the cops; and before I really could figure out what was happening, cop cars pulled up from every direction – three or four deep. I escaped that morning, running out through the back door before the police could exit their cars.

Three days later, while I was out trying to collect some money owed us on previous drug deals, my wife walked out, never to return. I had reached a new low. It didn't take long for me to realize that I never really was in love with her. And her actions following her departure made it very obvious that she wasn't in love with me, either.

A toxic relationship had finally come to an end. So I once again dove into the dope game, and deeper than ever before. Getting high was not enough; I wanted to get higher than I had ever been. I was moving more drugs around than ever. There were more girls than ever – I was with a

My Crystal Romance

different one virtually every night. Things got serious fast. Now, in addition to the drugs, there were guns, kidnappings, and thefts. Drug deals were not just local, but statewide. Heroin also entered the picture.

I stumbled across an old friend from 10 years earlier, and a unique connection for large drug quantities fell right into my lap. After recovering 2.2 pounds of stolen dope for him, he began to supply me with more meth than I had ever had in my life: $80,000 worth a week.

If you're wondering why I wasn't rich during this time, you have to understand how much I was spending to keep the flow of dope going. I was traveling from Alexandria to Shreveport to New

My Crystal Romance

Orleans to Lake Charles to Houston to keep my buyers supplied. I was staying in hotel rooms that cost $200 and $300 a night, not the local Motel 6. There were fancy cars, and even a $2,200-per-month condo in Houston.

One day, in the midst of all the high-rolling, I received a phone call from my mother. It was the worst news of my life, and one of the worst messages a father can ever receive about his child. "Brandon, your baby girl has leukemia." My entire world turned upside down at that moment.. But I was sitting in the driveway of a house, about to deliver a drug deal, when the call came in. I pressed the button and disconnected the call, put my phone in my pocket, and got out of the car and finished the deal I had come to make. That shows you how strong a meth addiction can be, as well as the lifestyle of dealing meth.

Throughout the coming year, I "arranged my schedule" to be at perhaps two of her chemo treatments. Others took her there, stayed with her, and held her hand through the treatments. They made her smile through her tears and were there for her. I, her father, was absent. Ady beat cancer. And here enters again the grace of mercy of God in my life because to that little girl, what matters isn't my absence then, but that I'm here now.

I remember that in 2015, depression, anger, fear, and hatred fueled a new level of use and dealing that I had never come close to before. I had lost my second wife and the respect of my whole family. I thought my kids didn't care about me anymore; I didn't blame them too much because I didn't care about myself that much, either. That has to be the most dangerous place a person can reach.

I started dealing more meth than ever, and found myself doing business with people for the first time who would kill me without hesitation for the slightest mistake or misstep. By sheer coincidence, I made it into a situation that sent me to a living room in Texas with members of a Mexican drug cartel. Instead of appreciating the danger and wanting out as soon as possible, my drug-damaged mind thought it was exactly where I wanted to be.

This meeting was different, though. Since it was my initial meeting, I was putting not only my own life, but also the lives of everyone I love in danger for this chance to be "the man". On this particular day, I had been shown enough meth to supply the whole south for about a week.

I was meeting with a cartel family about the terms of doing business with them. I remember going down there with $5,000, thinking it would impress them; and then feeling stupid when they didn't even entertain the possibility of letting me spend it that day. They told me it was no good that day because they wanted me to take the dope on the front (credit) with my family's safety as collateral. I don't remember even thinking twice about it. That shows you how sick a drug-addicted brain can be.

The gentleman brought me into a room and sat down with me at a computer, and began to show me where all my family lived; they even showed me where my current girlfriend got her nails done. The information they can acquire is probably as good as or better than that of the FBI.

Then the gentleman showed me a video I will never forget. Do you know how some people will pull up a video online and show you someone else doing something on camera? Well, I quickly noticed that this was a video of the man who was

My Crystal Romance

sitting next to me on the couch and showing me the video.

In the recording, he and a Mexican woman were casually talking while walking through a small field toward a barn. As they approached the barn, it was apparent that a large white man was lying on the ground and tied up. He was pleading for his life. The Mexican man totally ignored the man on the ground, continued his conversation with the woman, and simply took a blade from his pocket and cut the man's head off. I think what scared me the most about the situation, besides the obvious, was the fact that he never broke his conversation with the woman. It was bone-chilling cold.

My Crystal Romance

He clicked the video off. Then he turned to me, extended his hand to shake it in agreement, and said: "This is what happens to people who don't come back with my money."

At that moment, everything seemed to go into slow motion, as it does at that moment when your car starts spinning out of control before impact. I reached out, shook his hand, and agreed. In that second, the faces of the important people in my life flashed through my mind – my parents, my kids, and my girlfriend. I know I was doing something wrong and using a life lesson from my dad in an unintended way. However, I was thankful my dad had raised me to be honorable,

My Crystal Romance

and to keep my word. If I had not taken that lesson to heart, I probably would not be here.

I'll never forget the drive back to Louisiana from Texas. I had more meth in the car with me than ever before: 2 kilos, which is 2,000 grams or 4.4 pounds. It was so much that it couldn't be hidden, only covered. If I got stopped and caught with it, I would never get out of jail. But all I could think of was that if one thing went wrong, I would die behind the meth this time.

It had me so stressed and worried that I couldn't even sell any of it for about three days. I got back to Louisiana and used a little of it to pay someone to be my security, and I locked myself and him in a hotel room. I was afraid to come out, yet I knew

My Crystal Romance

I had to. This was enough meth that if the police caught me, the Mexican cartel would kill me. I had to sell it and get their money back to them as quickly as possible. I was so afraid of coming up short or being late in getting the money to them, I would sell it for barely more than what I paid for it. I was now risking my life and my family's safety, and taking more risks than ever for less money a week than what I could make on a $20-per-hour job.

I say that to try to get the point across: that the addiction to being important is so strong that even with the threat of death, it cannot be broken. I was so important to my family and my five daughters; but subconsciously, that was not important enough to matter. When you feel as though you are critical to people who are choosing you over others, it seems to overpower the importance you have to someone by default.

Another thing about the lifestyle that was so addictive was the fact that money wasn't important if you had meth. Because of the addition of the end user, the dealer could have anything he wanted as long as he could pay for it with meth. A person addicted to meth will steal anything for their next high, or trade anything he owns. I have gotten $5,000 dirt bikes in trade for what cost me $75 in meth. I'm not stating this to make dealing sound desirable. I'm saying this to show the extremes that an addict will take to get high. I have had men let me have their girlfriend for the night for meth, and the girl was happy to do it for meth as well.

I have tried to keep my writing as clean as I can because there is so much that I am ashamed of. I also have daughters who I know will read this one day. But I wouldn't be helping them or other women if I didn't include the degrading aspect of it. Meth is so powerful that it will take a girl who has always respected herself and her body or her significant other, and cause her to give herself in the most degrading way to a man. It will cause a man who was raised to respect women to take advantage of women at every opportunity.

My Crystal Romance

I tried to lie to myself and say I would never give a girl drugs for sex because I thought that was so sick and lowdown. I even went to the extreme of telling the girls I ended up alone with that we could get as high as she wanted, but sex was not expected in return. That was only to make myself feel better because I knew that would be the outcome every time.

CHAPTER 6

I was with more women in 2016 than I had ever been with throughout my whole life. Let me say this to those men who think that sounds like a dream come true: it's not! I lived every fantasy I ever had in my life, and was left in a very horrible place. Sex is a very wonderful thing when the time is right, and within the confines of a God-ordained marriage. Sex can and will be delightful and satisfying within that loving relationship. Outside of that, the misuse of and overindulgence in sex in drug-enhanced situations makes it anything but satisfying. It leaves you feeling empty and alone.

My Crystal Romance

As I go into a future clean of drugs and making my life count for the kingdom of God, I realize that God's law of reaping and sowing will still be in place. I allowed the enemy to take something from me that will be very hard to get back. It will be hard for me to have a happy and normal relationship without punishing a future woman for past women's behavior. I have built a wall that is so hard to tear down. I had to protect my own emotions during all of the sex and promiscuity that I am afraid I have lost the ability to have those emotions that make sex great, and make relationships alone great. I have gotten so used to "love" only being a 2- to 3-night thing that I learned to leave all emotion out, to just go through

My Crystal Romance

the words and motions. I wasn't sure if I truly could love or feel those emotions anymore.

I am so thankful that God has restored that in my life. I am praying and trusting that He will protect my five amazing daughters from this whole subject forever. Daddy loves you girls, and your God-given virtue is the most important thing you were born with. Guard it, save it, and respect it until you marry a man who will love you and respect it as much as you have. I pray that you will marry someone who will appreciate your body as a gift from God that he will work hard every day to earn the right to enjoy.

My Crystal Romance

I'll get back to where I was in the drug life because the things that led up to the end were nothing less than God's grace.

I never saw myself as anything more than the next guy. I felt desired, powerful and cool. But I never saw myself as influential to others. I never saw that I had such an effect on others and their actions. I only looked at myself through my own eyes, never realizing that I was leaving an unforgettable mark on everyone around me. It wasn't until I got to jail and rehab, and started having other people tell me about all the ways they remember me or I affected them.

I once told a friend that I never put a gun to anyone's head and made them get high. His response hit me hard. He said, "No, but you sure painted a beautiful picture of it." He said he had never known anyone who had so much passion in everything they did like I did, and that I made drugs and the lifestyle look so desirable. I never realized that while I was living through it.

It wasn't until I got to rehab with several people from my hometown that I started realizing my influence through the stories they told. There were even a few whom I didn't know, but had heard stories about me – true things I had no idea were spread all around the local drug community to people I didn't even know. I was so ashamed when I saw that so many people idolized me. Of all the legacies I could have left over the past 15 years, I'm so disappointed that it is the legacy of the dope game I chose.

That's when I realized I had to turn this writing into a book. Not only to say I'm sorry or ask for forgiveness, but to try to find a way to reach as many of those I led astray and do my best to pull them back in. I'm hoping that in telling my story, people will see there is no happy ending to it. Every single experience I have written about in this book led to pain. It is only by the grace of God and the prayers of an amazing prayer warrior mother (and the others who prayed for me) that none of my experiences resulted in my death.

I went to court in January of 2017 for a drug and distribution charge that was one of the biggest at that time. I was arrested with 100 grams of meth (over $7,000 worth), several pieces of paraphernalia, a good bit of cash, and a terrible attitude. They initially charged me with possession of meth (CDS II), distribution, trafficking, manufacturing, and possession of paraphernalia. I should be spending 30 years in jail right now; but God, in his grace, had another plan. He has allowed me a chance to change my life, and a chance to try to change the lives of all those I led astray.

I went to court on those charges; and my court-appointed attorney walked up to me and said they have dropped several of the charges, and are offering a two-year suspended sentence with two years' probation. I TOOK IT! I'm not going to do any time. Unfortunately, I didn't see it as a miracle at that point. It was a wake-up call, and it caused me to decide not to sell drugs anymore. However, it wasn't enough to make me quit using. That was God's first example of amazing grace in my new life.

What followed leading up to the point of me writing this book was nothing short of God's hand working His plan in my life. I left court that day saying, "That was close" and "I won't get that lucky again." In my mind, I wanted to get out of that life and never look back. I even called a local rehab and halfway house affiliated with my church and requested a bed. But I never showed up when they called because I was out trying to get high one more time before I went.

One month after being put on probation, God chose to pull me out since I couldn't do it myself. I was at a girlfriend's apartment, having someone give me a tattoo down my whole arm. After several hours of pain, I decided to take a break.

A few minutes into our break time, another friend stopped by and asked me to ride with him to find a stolen phone. I agreed to go so I'd have something to do. I didn't even know this guy well; I had only met him two days before.

God put me in that car with him that afternoon. Within two blocks of my girlfriend's apartment, we were swarmed by narcotics officers. I didn't have any drugs or paraphernalia on me; I hadn't sold any meth since being put on probation. I thought I was good. But God's plan was different than what I thought I knew. There was a distribution warrant on record with the police. I was arrested that day, which violated my probation.

God's grace put me in rehab. I was sent to the first program where, for the first time in 41 years, I received an actual revelation of God's grace toward me. I began to realize and somehow know in my heart and mind that what Christ did for me on the cross was enough. For 41 years, I had been taught that I had to work for my salvation. I believed that after I received the Holy Spirit and accepted Christ into my life, all I had to do was live right, stay "prayed through", and continually go to Him for forgiveness. Regardless of how much of that is true in concept, without an understanding of grace being the unmerited favor of God – emphasizing unmerited favor – the enemy can continually make us feel we are not good enough, not saved enough, and never will be. He makes giving up seem like the only route available to us. His lies are a part of his plan to destroy us, both spiritually and literally.

In those first two months of rehab, I finally saw God's grace, and recognized that what Jesus did on the cross saved me. It was and will always be sufficient. "For where sin doth abound, grace doth much more abound" (Romans 5:20). That passage talks about all sin: past, present, and future. I finally understood through God's Word that when I surrender my life to Christ and truly receive Him as my Savior, my faith in what He did on the cross for me will get me all the way to heaven. Grace will keep me from sin. And if I do sin, grace allows me access to repentance and restoration. Sin is not the end of our story; grace is.

We are all human; and we are prone to the sins, faults, and failures that come with that. None of us will ever, on our own, be good enough. The scripture says, "All we like sheep have gone astray…" (Isaiah 53:6). The important thing to know is that God does not expect us to come to

Him in a state of perfection. The Message version of 2 Corinthians 5:21 says this: "God put the wrong on him who never did anything wrong, so we could be put right with God." Jesus Christ knew no sin, yet He became sin so that we could be free from sin.

What Christ did for me 2,000 years ago was once and for all enough to save me. My faith in Him and what He did will save me. The most important thing I learned there was that what Christ did for me on the cross to purchase my salvation was a finished work. My faith in that finished work is what allows me to stand before God in righteousness that comes only from God. My righteousness – the things I would do and say to try somehow to make myself appear good and worthy – are, before God, just "filthy rags". The fact is that only because He took my sin and gave me His righteousness am I righteous at all.

I hope and fervently pray that what I have said in this book will be the thing that inspires someone to come to Christ, and let me remain an example to those around me and lead them to Christ. It truly is a better life.

CHAPTER 7

One night, while I was well into my addiction (and about three years before I got clean), I had an experience that was miraculous. I had a habit at the time of going outside every morning, well before daylight; and sitting there alone, watching the shadow figures created by the moonlight and clouds until the sun came up.

I remember a particular Sunday morning. At about five o'clock am, while sitting there in the dark alone, something besides imaginary shadow figures captured my attention. Looking at the property behind my house, I saw what looked like

My Crystal Romance

five columns of smoke going around the back of my property, and extending to the front.

I called my wife out, and asked her if she saw them. She said, "Man, you're just high and seeing things."

She went back inside; and I sat there and watched these columns all the way until daylight, and they faded away. I went in and began to go on with my day, just writing off what I saw as a hallucination.

At about 8:30 am, my phone rang. It was my mother. She was calling to invite me to the church that morning. What she said after that sent chills and goosebumps down my spine. Knowing nothing about what I had just seen, she said:

"Brandon, I want you to know that God woke me up at 5 this morning, thinking about you. I hit my knees and began to pray that God would put pillars of protection around you, your family and home." It shook me to the bone. My mom will hear about this happening for the first time when she reads this book.

In early 2018, I was released from a residential rehab program in Logansport, Louisiana and remanded to the Rapides Parish Jail. I was not sure what exactly would be the outcome of my situation. After meetings with my attorney and the assigned judge, I was released to a residential program for homeless men that was operated by a local church; and ultimately, into the care and keeping of my beloved parents.

As I am writing this, I am currently enrolled at the Louisiana Association of Substance Abuse Counselors and Trainers (LASACT), pursuing certification as a substance abuse counselor. I hope my future will bring employment as a drug counselor so I can help other young men and women change their lives before their addiction destroys as much of their lives as it did mine.

I sit here a year and a half after I wrote this book, pondering this last chapter's content. I sit here a completely different man than who I was when I initially started writing this book, all because of the fact that God has done so much for me since the first day I sat down and started to write.

First, let me start by explaining how this journey began. While in rehab back in September 2017, I was constantly beating myself up over my past. I replayed these memories over and over in my head, to the point that it was driving me crazy. One day, I decided I just needed to get it all out, and thought that my best outlet would be to write it all down. Before writing the first word, I committed to fully and ultimately telling the truth: "The whole truth and nothing but the truth." The first memory I could recall was written first.

This book was originally intended to be honest and revealing because I never meant for anyone

My Crystal Romance

to read it. It was initially intended to be a cleansing of mind and soul for my mental well-being. I wrote everything I could remember. Then I closed the notebook and put it away. At some point, over the following weeks, God started dealing with me about being transparent and telling my family the truth about my past in an effort to try and compensate for all the lies I had told them for years.

So, I sent what I had written home for them to read. After their initial shock of reading the details had worn off, I was eventually asked if they could let someone else read it.

Long story short, here we are.

I need to bring you up to speed on where God has brought me to now. I am sitting here next to my beautiful wife that God has given me. We are discussing all the miracles in our lives that have come about since I returned home from rehab thirteen months ago. When I came home, I had a God-given burden to help others who are struggling with addiction. I had finally decided to commit to following God's plan for my life, no matter where he took me. It is an amazing journey!

God has opened so many doors since I began to follow the paths He set before me. The Bible says, "His word is a lamp unto our feet and a light unto our path." He lights our paths the way ahead

My Crystal Romance

of us while also giving a specific guiding light through a lamp at our feet. I have never lived in more blessings than since I started following each step He lays before me.

I decided that the best way I could follow God's plan for my life was to go to school to be a substance abuse counselor. I graduate next month from substance abuse counselor training. I cannot wait to see where God takes me in that avenue.

My goal is to open a faith-based, long-term rehab facility. However, I could not see it ever happening financially. God stepped in and started opening doors. He placed me in front of one person after another who held the keys to each door I needed to open to pursue this dream. I have now started "BETHESDA HOUSE", a sober-living house with funding God provided. With this, I will also be able to raise the money to follow my calling to open a rehab center. I am so blessed.

Recovery? I have recovered everything the devil ever took from me. I have covered more new ground than ever before in my life. I have my kids back and living at home with me, and I have a beautiful wife who loves and follows God. I can work with addicts every day to try to help them find the blessings in God that come with sobriety and dedicating your life to Him.

My Crystal Romance

FINAL WORDS OF THANKS

So many important people have been instrumental in this process. I wish I could name them all; you know who you are. I thank you all. I thank my beautiful wife, Natalie Nicole Chatagnier, for standing by my side, following me as we follow Christ.

Mom, thank you again for praying for me. Your prayers were being answered all along. Thank you for not losing faith and not giving up. I love you. Thank you for being an example and a prayer warrior. Thank you, Dad, for always expecting more, for always knowing I could be better. God uses your voice to call out the best in me. Keep calling; by God's grace, I will keep striving to be more like Him – and more like you.

My special thanks to my five amazing daughters: Magan, Haley, Alyssa, Patience, and Ady. Despite my absence from your life, and without the influence of a Godly father, you still were smart enough and brave enough to choose to live for God, to keep praying for me. I am humbled that despite all my failings, you still want to call me "Daddy" – and still let me be your hero.

Finally, I give thanks to Jesus Christ for His grace and mercy toward me. I thank Him for dying for me on the cross of Calvary. I thank Him for forgiving me all my sins, washing them away into a sea of forgetfulness. I thank Him for filling me with the Holy Spirit, and allowing me to walk with him for the rest of my days. None of this could have been done without him. I did none of this; this was all done by God through me. My God is amazing. I am reaping the benefits of a life submitted to him, and His will and work in me.

Thank you for being curious enough to open up this book and take the time to read it. If you are an addict, may you find hope to seek the freedom that can only come through Jesus Christ. If you love an addict, may you find hope that helps you keep praying for God's deliverance to come to your house. It's on its way!

My Crystal Romance

THE END

Made in the USA
Monee, IL
08 May 2023